SPORTS SUPERSTARS

SIDNEY CROSBY

BY INDIA JAMES

BELLWETHER MEDIA • MINNEAPOLIS, MN

TORQUE

Torque brims with excitement perfect for thrill-seekers of all kinds. Discover daring survival skills, explore uncharted worlds, and marvel at mighty engines and extreme sports. In *Torque* books, anything can happen. Are you ready?

This edition first published in 2025 by Bellwether Media, Inc.

No part of this publication may be reproduced in whole or in part without written permission of the publisher. For information regarding permission, write to Bellwether Media, Inc., Attention: Permissions Department, 6012 Blue Circle Drive, Minnetonka, MN 55343.

Library of Congress Cataloging-in-Publication Data

LC record for Sidney Crosby available at: https://lccn.loc.gov/2024047002

Text copyright © 2025 by Bellwether Media, Inc. TORQUE and associated logos are trademarks and/or registered trademarks of Bellwether Media, Inc.

Editor: Kieran Downs   Designer: Gabriel Hilger

Printed in the United States of America, North Mankato, MN.

TABLE OF CONTENTS

SCORE!	4
WHO IS SIDNEY CROSBY?	6
EARLY ON THE ICE	8
TROPHIES AND GOLD MEDALS	12
CROSBY'S FUTURE	20
GLOSSARY	22
TO LEARN MORE	23
INDEX	24

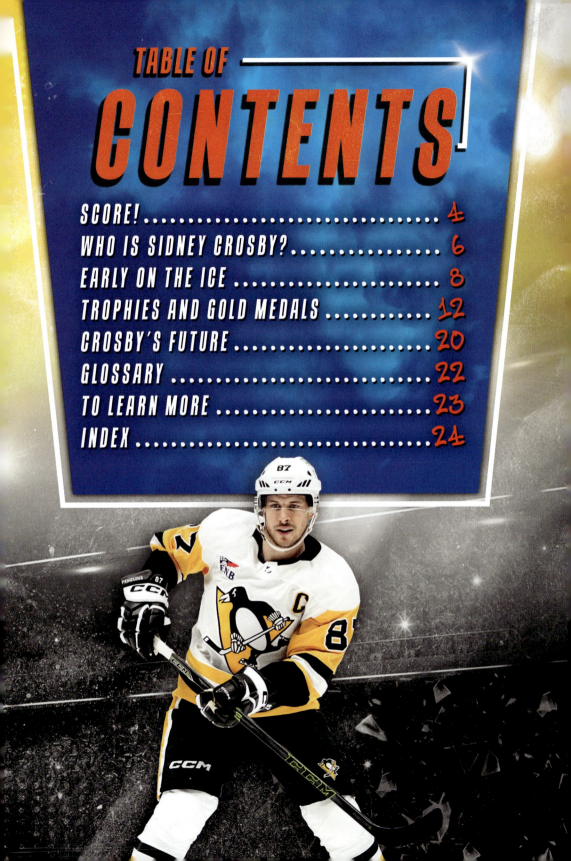

SCORE!

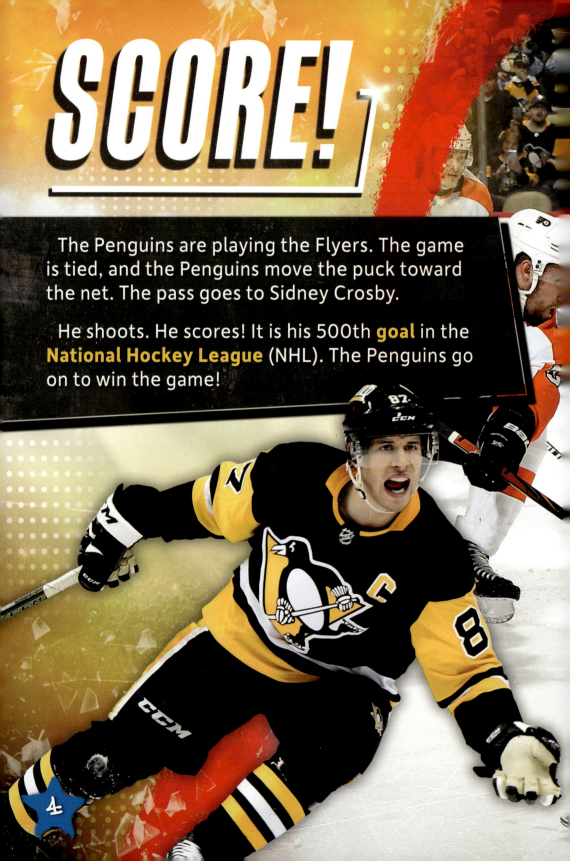

The Penguins are playing the Flyers. The game is tied, and the Penguins move the puck toward the net. The pass goes to Sidney Crosby.

He shoots. He scores! It is his 500th **goal** in the **National Hockey League** (NHL). The Penguins go on to win the game!

WHO IS SIDNEY CROSBY?

Sidney Crosby is a **professional** hockey player. He plays **center** for the Pittsburgh Penguins. He is known for scoring many points.

Leader of the Pack

Crosby became captain of the Penguins in 2007. He was the youngest captain in NHL history.

SIDNEY CROSBY

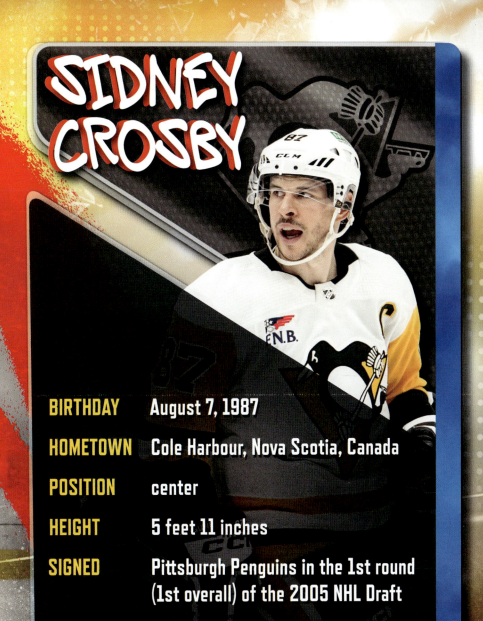

BIRTHDAY	August 7, 1987
HOMETOWN	Cole Harbour, Nova Scotia, Canada
POSITION	center
HEIGHT	5 feet 11 inches
SIGNED	Pittsburgh Penguins in the 1st round (1st overall) of the 2005 NHL Draft

Crosby has won many awards. He has won the **Hart Memorial Trophy** twice. He has won the **Stanley Cup** three times. He has also won two gold medals for Canada in the **Winter Olympics**.

EARLY ON THE ICE

Crosby was born in Canada. He learned about hockey when he was very young. His dad was a hockey player. Crosby had learned to skate by the time he was 3 years old.

CROSBY WITH FAMILY

COLE HARBOUR, CANADA

Crosby played on many hockey teams as a kid. He showed his talent at a young age. He scored 159 goals in 55 games when he was 10 years old!

Crosby moved from Canada to the United States during high school. He helped his team win a **championship**. He moved back to Canada after one year.

Crosby played in the Quebec Major **Junior** Hockey League. He scored 135 points in one year. He also became the youngest player to score a goal at the World Junior Championships.

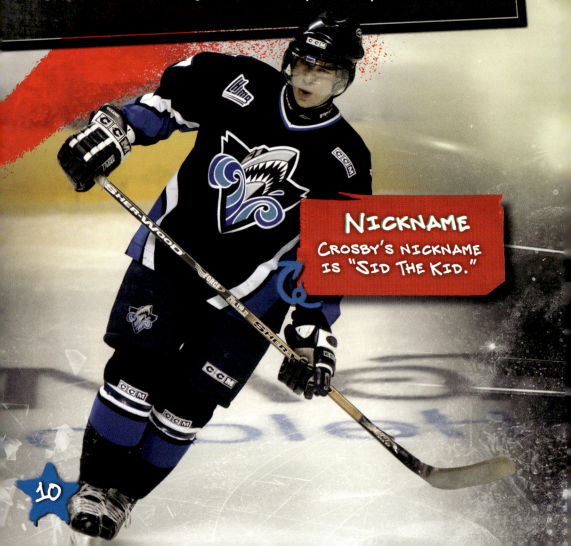

NICKNAME
Crosby's nickname is "Sid the Kid."

FAVORITES

ICE CREAM
cookie dough

KARAOKE SONG
"Don't Stop Believin'" by Journey

CANDY
Reese's Peanut Butter Cups

FOOD
Italian

TROPHIES AND GOLD MEDALS

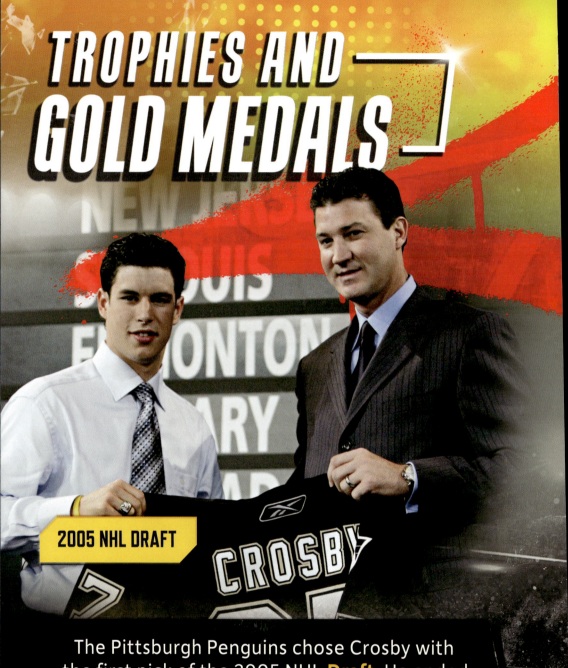

2005 NHL DRAFT

The Pittsburgh Penguins chose Crosby with the first pick of the 2005 NHL **Draft**. He ended his first season with 102 points.

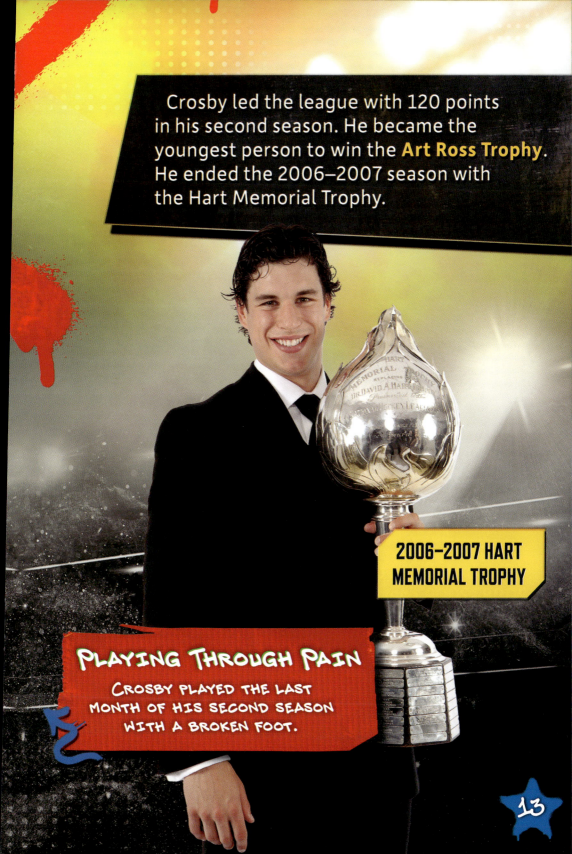

Crosby led the league with 120 points in his second season. He became the youngest person to win the **Art Ross Trophy**. He ended the 2006–2007 season with the Hart Memorial Trophy.

2006–2007 HART MEMORIAL TROPHY

Playing Through Pain

Crosby played the last month of his second season with a broken foot.

2008–2009 STANLEY CUP

Crosby helped the Penguins win in the 2008–2009 season. They made it to the **playoffs** and won the Stanley Cup. Crosby played for Team Canada in the 2010 Vancouver Winter Olympics. He scored the winning goal in the gold medal game!

In 2011, Crosby got a **concussion**. He struggled with recovery for a few seasons.

SIDNEY CROSBY MAP

● Pittsburgh Penguins, Pittsburgh, Pennsylvania

2005 to present

2010 VANCOUVER WINTER OLYMPICS

A Good Year

Crosby was born on August 7, 1987. He wears number 87 because of this.

Crosby was healthy during the 2013–2014 season. He played well and won the Hart Memorial Trophy for the second time. He also won his second Art Ross Trophy.

Crosby helped Team Canada win gold at the 2014 Sochi Winter Olympics. He led the Penguins to two more Stanley Cup titles in 2015–2016 and 2016–2017.

2014 SOCHI WINTER OLYMPICS

TAPING TRICK

Crosby does not let anyone touch his stick before a game after he has taped it. If someone does, he puts new tape on the stick.

Crosby helped the Penguins reach the playoffs in 2017–2018. They lost in the second round. The Penguins also reached the playoffs in 2018–2019 but did not win. During the season, Crosby scored 100 points!

Crosby hurt his wrist in the 2021–2022 season. But he played every game of the 2022–2023 and 2023–2024 seasons.

TIMELINE

— 2005 —
Crosby is drafted by the Penguins

— 2009 —
Crosby wins his first Stanley Cup with the Penguins

— 2010 —
Crosby wins a gold medal at the 2010 Vancouver Winter Olympics

— 2014 —
Crosby wins a gold medal at the 2014 Sochi Winter Olympics

— 2017 —
Crosby wins his third Stanley Cup with the Penguins

CROSBY'S FUTURE

In 2009, Crosby started the Sidney Crosby **Foundation**. This group gives money to organizations that help children in the U.S. and Canada.

The Penguins have signed Crosby to stay with their team through 2027. He wants to keep playing hockey. He hopes to help his team win another Stanley Cup!

GLOSSARY

Art Ross Trophy—an award given to the scoring champion of an NHL season

center—a position in hockey where a player mostly stays in the middle of the ice

championship—a contest to decide the best team or person

concussion—a head injury that requires a player to rest for a long time

draft—a process during which professional teams choose high school and college players to play for them

foundation—an organization that helps people and communities

goal—a score in hockey; a player scores a goal by putting the puck into the other team's net.

Hart Memorial Trophy—an award given to the best player in an NHL season

junior—related to a competition between young people

National Hockey League—a professional hockey league in the United States and Canada; the National Hockey League is often called the NHL.

playoffs—games played after the regular season is over; playoff games determine which teams play in the championship game.

professional—related to a player or team that makes money playing a sport

Stanley Cup—the award for winning the championship series of the NHL

Winter Olympics—a worldwide winter sports contest held in a different country every four years

TO LEARN MORE

AT THE LIBRARY

Adamson, Thomas K. *Connor McDavid*. Minneapolis, Minn.: Bellwether Media, 2024.

Anderson, Josh. *Sidney Crosby vs. Wayne Gretzky: Who Would Win?* Minneapolis, Minn.: Lerner Publications, 2024.

Fishman, Jon M. *Hockey's G.O.A.T.: Wayne Gretzky, Sidney Crosby, and More*. Minneapolis, Minn.: Lerner Publications, 2020.

ON THE WEB

Factsurfer.com gives you a safe, fun way to find more information.

1. Go to www.factsurfer.com

2. Enter "Sidney Crosby" into the search box and click 🔍.

3. Select your book cover to see a list of related content.

INDEX

Art Ross Trophy, 13, 16
awards, 7, 13, 16
Canada, 7, 8, 9, 10, 14, 16, 20
captain, 6
center, 6
championship, 10
childhood, 8, 9, 10
draft, 12
family, 8
favorites, 11
goal, 4, 9, 10, 14
Hart Memorial Trophy, 7, 13, 16
hurt, 13, 14, 18
map, 15
National Hockey League, 4, 6, 12
nickname, 10
number, 15
Pittsburgh Penguins, 4, 6, 12, 14, 16, 18, 21
playoffs, 14, 18
points, 6, 10, 12, 13, 18
profile, 7
Quebec Major Junior Hockey League, 10
records, 6, 10, 13
Sidney Crosby Foundation, 20
Stanley Cup, 7, 14, 16, 17, 21
timeline, 18–19
trophy shelf, 17
United States, 10, 20
Winter Olympics, 7, 14, 15, 16
World Junior Championships, 10

The images in this book are reproduced through the courtesy of: Tony Gutierrez, cover, pp. 3, 7 (Sidney Crosby); Emilee Chinn/ Stringer/ Getty Images, p. 4; Joe Sargent/ Contributor/ Getty Images, p. 5; Bruce Bennett/ Staff/ Getty Images, pp. 6, 15 (2010 Vancouver Winter Olympics), 16, 19; Dave Sandford/ Contributor/ Getty Images, pp. 8, 20; Coastal Elite/ Wikipedia, p. 9; JACQUES BOISSINOT/ AP Images, pp. 10, 11 (Sidney Crosby); P Maxwell Photography, p. 11 (cookie dough); Blueee77, p. 11 ("Don't Stop Believin'"); mikeledray, p. 11 (Reese's Peanut Butter Cups); FotosDo, p. 11 (Italian); JONATHAN HAYWARD/ AP Images, p. 12; Graig Abel/ Stringer/ Getty Images, p. 13; Gregory Shamus/ Contributor/ Getty Images, p. 14; George Wirt, p. 15 (Pittsburgh Penguins logo); Mario Jose Sanchez/ AP Images, p. 17; Gene J. Puskar/ AP Images, p. 18; Pittsburgh Penguins/ Wikipedia, p. 18 (Pittsburgh Penguins logo); Jim McIsaac/ Staff/ Getty Images, p. 18 (2009); dpa picture alliance archive/ Alamy, p. 19 (2010); Grinchenkova Anzhela, p. 19 (2014); Mark Humphrey/ AP Images, p. 19 (2017); Icon Sportswire/ Contributor/ Getty Images, p. 21; Seth Wenig/ AP Images, p. 23.